SOCIAL SCIENCE

Mountain Climbing:
Dangerous and Deadly

MICHÈLE DUFRESNE

TABLE OF CONTENTS

Beautiful but Sometimes Deadly 2
"Because It's There" 4
The Thrill of the Climb 7
Climbing to Build Relationships 10
Climbing for Fun 12
A Changing Sport 14
Glossary/Index 20

PIONEER VALLEY EDUCATIONAL PRESS, INC

BEAUTIFUL BUT SOMETIMES DEADLY

K2, the second-highest mountain in the world, rises 28,251 feet into the air. Its white peak gleams in the sunshine and appears to touch the sky.

But this mountain is both beautiful and deadly. For every three people who reach its peak, another climber dies. Even the easiest route to the **summit** involves crossing a glacier and taking a path around a series of ice pillars that may collapse without warning.

The local name for K2 is *Chogori*, which means "king of mountains."

So why do climbers do it? Why risk your life to climb a mountain?

MORE TO EXPLORE

The weather on K2 is **VERY UNPREDICTABLE.** After being taken away on a stretcher with frostbitten feet, a climber named George Bell wrote, "It's a savage mountain that tries to kill you."

"BECAUSE IT'S THERE"

George Mallory was a famous **mountaineer** from England. In the 1920s, he attempted to climb Mount Everest, the tallest mountain in the world, three times. When someone asked him why he wanted to climb Mount Everest, he answered, "Because it's there."

GEORGE MALLORY

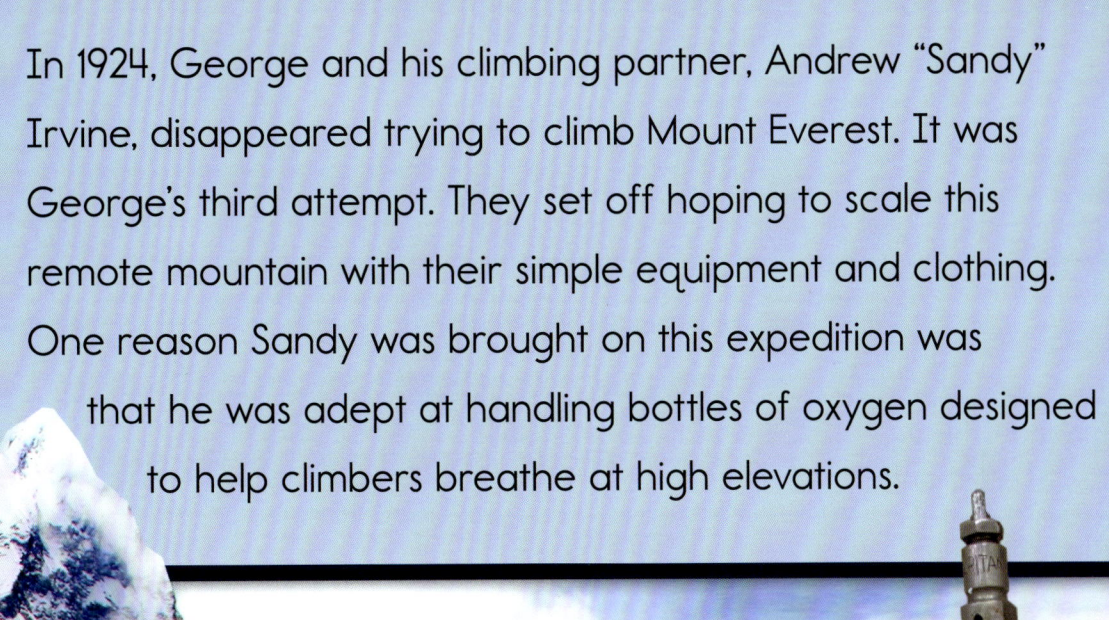

In 1924, George and his climbing partner, Andrew "Sandy" Irvine, disappeared trying to climb Mount Everest. It was George's third attempt. They set off hoping to scale this remote mountain with their simple equipment and clothing. One reason Sandy was brought on this expedition was that he was adept at handling bottles of oxygen designed to help climbers breathe at high elevations.

MORE TO EXPLORE

George Mallory previously thought that using oxygen bottles was "unsporting." But by his **THIRD CLIMB**, he finally came around to the idea that the tanks would be necessary to successfully reach the summit.

The team waiting at base camp last saw the two men about 800 feet from the summit. Right after, a sudden snow **squall** moved in, and it became impossible to see the upper part of the mountain. George and Sandy were never seen alive again.

George's body was finally discovered in 1999, but we will never know if he reached the top of the mountain. Were George and Sandy the first to summit the highest mountain in the world? Did they die on their way down, or were they still trying to get to the top when they died? Was there an **avalanche**, or did they run out of air? We can't know for sure.

> "One must conquer, achieve, get to the top; one must know the end to be convinced that one can win the end—to know there's no dream that mustn't be dared."
>
> —GEORGE MALLORY

THE THRILL OF THE CLIMB

People like George Mallory climb mountains because of the challenge. They dare to risk everything, including death, to accomplish their goal. They enjoy the challenge of scrambling up steep rocks and over slippery ice and snow to reach the summit.

The extreme cold at the peaks of these mountains can cause frostbite and **hypothermia**. There are peaks so high that the atmosphere has less oxygen, making it hard to breathe. Climbers must risk their lives to get to the tops of these mountains.

MORE TO EXPLORE

Many Sherpa people are excellent mountaineers and have guided others as they climb very **HIGH MOUNTAINS**, especially Mount Everest. Reaching the peak is extremely difficult without their help.

Cold is not the only risk climbers face; mountains can also expose humans to many other dangers. At extreme heights, a simple mistake can lead to injury or even death.

For instance, the ice and snow covering the surface of a mountain can pose many dangers for climbers. Snow can camouflage deep cracks in the ice, creating a snowbridge. These areas can appear solid but may only be a few inches thick, not nearly strong enough to walk on. Climbers cannot always tell when a snowbridge lies in front of them. Stepping on one could result in a fall into a **crevasse**.

The weather and environment can present dangers too. A sudden rainstorm might cover the trail with sleet, making the ground too slippery to cross. Melting ice can cause rocks to fall, while an avalanche of snow may bury anyone in its path.

Do all these dangers make climbing the tallest mountains in the world worthwhile? Some people think so.

MORE TO EXPLORE

In 2014, 13-year-old Poorna Malavath became the youngest girl to ever **CLIMB TO THE TOP** of Mount Everest. When asked why she attempted such a difficult and dangerous feat, she said she wanted to prove that "girls can achieve anything."

CLIMBING TO BUILD RELATIONSHIPS

Teamwork is an essential part of climbing. In frightening and dangerous situations, climbers must rely on other mountaineers.

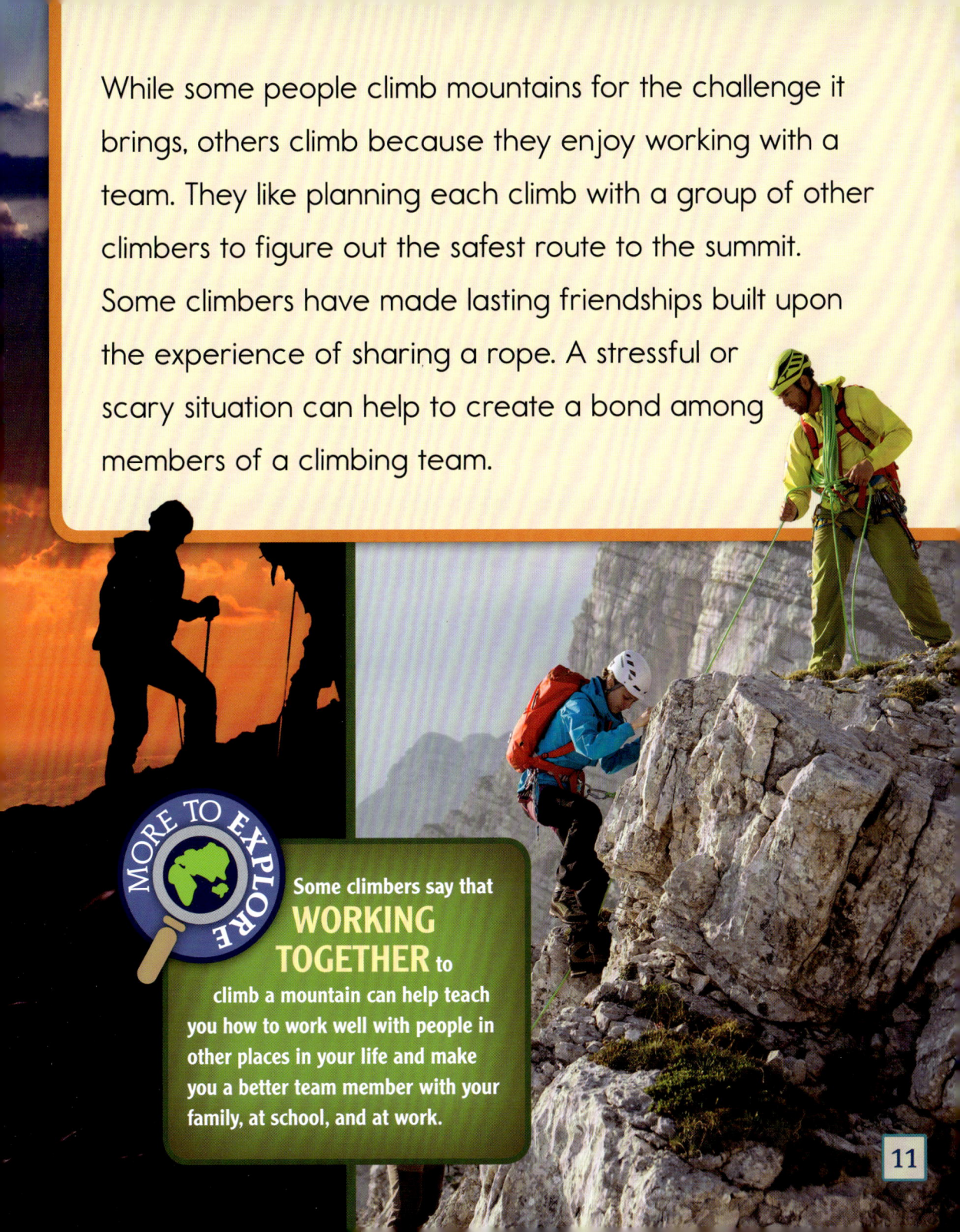

While some people climb mountains for the challenge it brings, others climb because they enjoy working with a team. They like planning each climb with a group of other climbers to figure out the safest route to the summit. Some climbers have made lasting friendships built upon the experience of sharing a rope. A stressful or scary situation can help to create a bond among members of a climbing team.

MORE TO EXPLORE

Some climbers say that **WORKING TOGETHER** to climb a mountain can help teach you how to work well with people in other places in your life and make you a better team member with your family, at school, and at work.

CLIMBING FOR FUN

Not everyone is looking for a dangerous challenge. Some people climb mountains simply for fun. Mount Rainier National Park in Washington has been keeping records on the number of climbers on the mountain since 1950. In the years since then, the number of people to climb Mount Rainier has gone from 238 to more than 10,000 annually. Why are more and more people climbing?

Many people climb mountains like Mount Rainier for the experience. At the summit, they can look out over the amazing vista, where they are higher than the surrounding cities and towns. From the tops of these small, fun, easy-to-climb mountains, a climber can see for miles in every direction and take in the beauty of our world.

Mount Rainier in Reflection Lake

People also enjoy the physical challenges involved with climbing. In fact, people enjoy climbing so much that indoor climbing gyms have sprung up around the world. At a climbing gym, everyone from a novice to an experienced climber can climb in a safe place year-round. Climbing gyms offer classes to get you started and are even popular for children's birthday parties.

Climbing walls can be found in more than 140 countries around the world!

A CHANGING SPORT

Mountain climbing has changed quite a bit since the early days of the sport. Back then, a climber might have had nothing more than a few ropes. Today there is new equipment that can help make climbing easier and safer.

MORE TO EXPLORE

In 1953, an **EXPEDITION TO THE SUMMIT** of Mount Everest used wireless radios that only worked on the lower part of the mountain. Today climbers can sometimes make cell phone calls from the summit.

To keep warm, early climbers wore layers of wool and bulky boots. They slept in tents made of heavy cotton that they had to haul up the mountain. If it rained, their clothes became waterlogged, making the climb much tougher.

Climbers today wear down-filled suits that they both climb and sleep in. Boots are waterproof and insulated from the cold. And tents are made of lightweight fabric that's both easy to carry and resistant to frigid temperatures and high winds.

climbing boots

tents

In 1924, to help with the thin atmosphere near the top of Mount Everest, George Mallory carried heavy tanks of oxygen. He also carried a special tool called an altimeter to measure the height of his climb. Climbers today carry lightweight oxygen tanks and wear watches that not only measure altitude but also aid in navigation.

Early climbers tied a simple rope around themselves to help prevent falls. Today climbers use harnesses that can absorb the shock from a fall.

crampons

Long ago, climbers used an ice ax to anchor into ice or hard snow. Climbers today still use ice axes, but modern axes have become much smaller and more lightweight.

To help provide **traction** on snow and ice, mountain climbers have long used metal plates strapped to the bottoms of their boots. Early crampons were very heavy and had four simple spikes. Today's crampons are lightweight and have ten to twelve points.

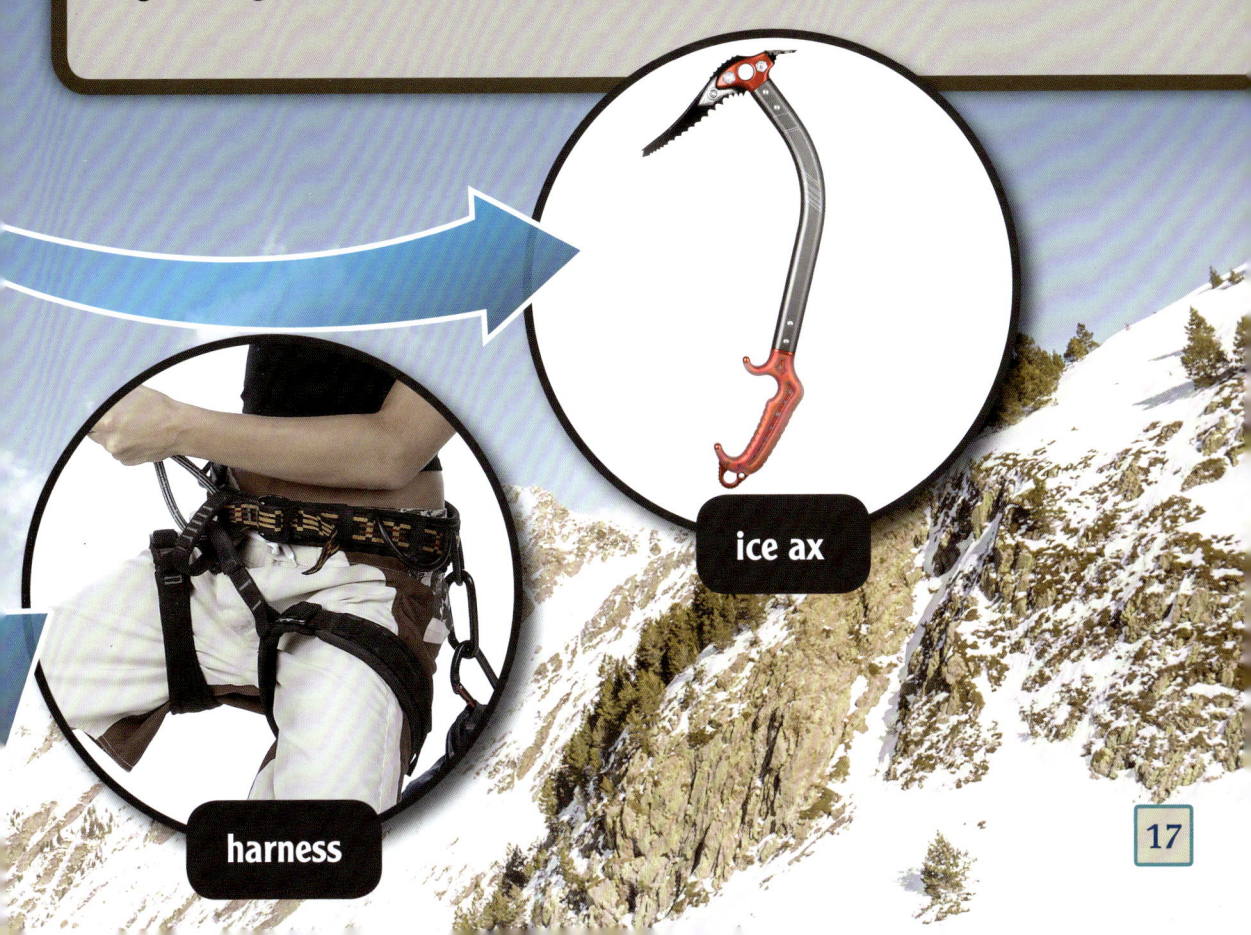

ice ax

harness

Even with the best equipment and years of training, mountain climbing is still a very dangerous sport. The weather can change in a moment, bringing wind, snow, and ice that could turn a fun activity into a disaster.

MORE TO EXPLORE

Climbers in snowy areas should bring shovels, radios, an emergency beacon, and long poles for **FINDING PEOPLE** who have been buried in the snow.

GLOSSARY

avalanche
a large amount of snow or rocks that slides suddenly down the side of a mountain

crevasse
a deep, narrow opening or crack in an area of thick ice or rock

hypothermia
a dangerous condition in which the body temperature is brought to an extreme low

mountaineer
a mountain climber

squall
a sudden violent wind, often with rain, sleet, or snow

summit
the top of a mountain

traction
the ability to stick to a surface while still being able to move

INDEX

altimeter 16
Andrew "Sandy" Irvine 5–6
atmosphere 7, 16
avalanche 6, 9
boots 15, 17
Chogori 2
climbing gym 13
climbing walls 13
crampons 16–17
crevasse 8
dangers 8–9
equipment 5, 14, 18
frostbite 7
George Bell 3
George Mallory 4–6, 7, 16
harness 16–17
hypothermia 7
ice 2, 7, 8–9, 17, 18, 20
ice ax 17
K2 2–3
Mount Everest 4–5, 7, 9, 14, 16
Mount Rainier 12
mountaineer 4, 7, 10
oxygen 5, 7, 16
Poorna Malavath 9
risk 3, 7, 8
Sherpa 7
snowbridge 8
squall 6
summit 2, 5, 6, 7, 11, 12, 14
teamwork 10
tents 15
traction 17
weather 3, 9, 18

The DEADLIEST Mounta

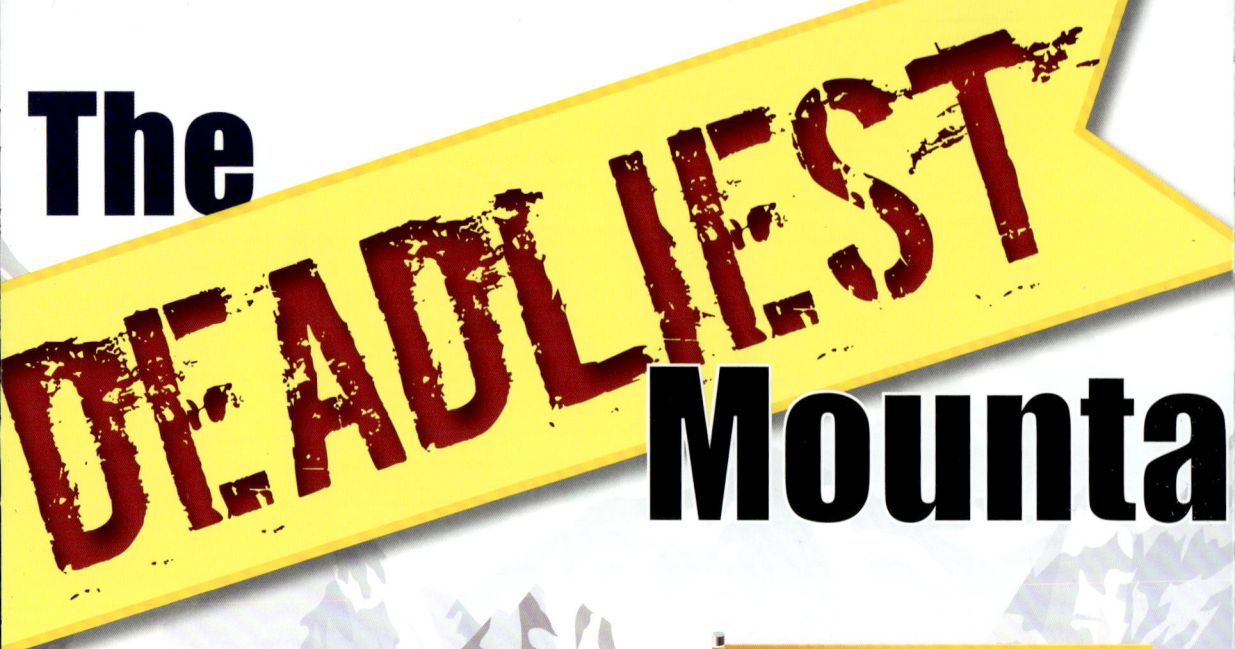

1. Annapurna

Annapurna is the world's most dangerous mountain. Almost half its climbers have died in the attempt, most of them during sudden snowstorms or avalanches.

3. Nanga Parbat

Nanga Parbat has an enormous ridge of ice and rock that makes it so perilous to climb that it has been nicknamed the "Man Eater."

2. K2

K2 has steep slopes and bad weather that make it the second-most deadly mountain to climb.

ins in the World

Switzerland
Pakistan
Nepal

5. The Eiger

The Eiger challenges climbers with many hazards, including falling rocks. Its north face has been nicknamed "Murder Wall."

6. The Matterhorn

The Matterhorn is a beautiful mountain that looks like a horn rising out of the surrounding valleys. Avalanches, rockfalls, and overcrowding from too many hikers have led to many deaths on this mountain.

4. Kangchenjunga

Kangchenjunga is dangerous to climb because of avalanches and bad weather.

But as long as there are mountains, there will be people to climb them—simply because they are there!